This Life:
a love story

Maryalicia Post

Acknowledgment

Acknowledgment is made to these magazines and journals where many of these poems first appeared: the cherita, Atlas Poetica, moonbathing, Ribbons, Pangolin Review, Poetry Quarterly. And to this book : ARC (Maryalicia Post) Independently published and available from Amazon.

With thanks to the poet ai li

who devised the six-line poetry form in 1997

and christened it 'cherita'

the Malay word for 'story'.

Contents

My father setting the clock to daylight savings, Autumn

He lifts down the clock
from the shelf in the dining room
and places it on a clean tea cloth
on the big table

With his thumbnail
he flicks the little golden latch
and the glass falls forward
on its tiny hinges

We see the clock's radiant face
like a bride's with her veil thrown back
and the butterfly-intricate hands
breathless, I watch

 The minute hand, pressed down,
turns steadily 'clockwise'
not back an hour but
eleven slow turns forward.

Time moves in only one direction
 it cannot be turned back
He wanted me to know -
I know it now

I'll take you home again
Kathleen
singing with my father

sitting on the back steps
evening scent
of honeysuckle

The Depression had recently hit the USA and my family and Jack's were among those who settled in a badly built building on the harbour front in Brooklyn to wait for Roosevelt's 'New Deal' to take hold so we could all move on and up.

In the summer nights, when heat smothered every room, Jack's family and mine would meet on the roof of the building. The adults sat on kitchen chairs they'd brought up from their apartments, the women in their light summer dresses fanning themselves in the dark. The heat of the day would have softened the roof's tarpaper covering, its oily smell mixing with the fresh scent of salt drifting in on the breeze from the harbour. Over the roof's parapet we could see the lights on the masts of the ships and nearer still the vacant lot in which my father's car was abandoned.

I remember a garden

when I was
 young

where my parents
laughed
and I picked peonies

Too late

To say I'm sorry
Now I'm grown

Walking the same path
On which you stumbled

Jack was eight, He would sit with his back against the coping of the roof, his knees drawn up to his chest. I would sit next to him wherever he settled; close enough to feel his warmth, as alive to his movement as a cat. I was four years old, and though I didn't know the word yet, I had fallen in love with him when he helped me out of a tree - in full view of the neighbourhood boys who would mock him unceasingly. I knew he was his own man, then, kind and brave. I would never stop loving him. To me, Owl's Head was the heart of the world, especially because Jack and his family lived upstairs, for I not only loved Jack, I loved his family as well. Then one evening at the end of summer my mother told us that Jack's family was moving away.

wild water

spraying from the hydrant
gushing in the gutter

summer smells of dust
and tar
childhood, Brooklyn

at the street corner

an old man warns me
not to cross against the light

I wait and feel
my long-gone mother's hand hold mine
until red turns to green

"They're off to a house of their own," she said. "A house with a lawn.In New Jersey' .She   seemed slightly offended. My father put down his newspaper and looked up at her. . I'll be…!' he said. He sounded really surprised. I wasn't surprised. They had always seemed too special to share our life for good. More like royalty visiting.

And now they were going.

They had dinner with us the night before they left. The kitchen table had been spread with a white tablecloth and the bridge lamp had been brought in from the sitting room. This was a floor lamp with a decorative metal arm, the bridge, from which a shaded bulb dangled. It was drawn up to the table and like a congenial extra guest beamed down impartially on the dishes and the knives and forks. But it wasn't a festive evening. In the bridge lamp's unfamiliar light we all looked solemn. We were solemn.

corner store

butter in tubs
milk by the can

rubber boots
dangling from the ceiling
dust

biscuits

all the same
different shapes

the flower-patterned
ones
taste best

On those long twilight evenings on the roof, Arthur had described one moneymaking idea or another to my father. while my father made jokes. Now one of Arthurs' plans had worked and my father seemed to have lost his sense of humour. May and my mother passed the platters and dishes whenever there was a silence. My little sister had fallen asleep on the sofa before dinner was ready, her blond curls heat-pasted to her rosy cheek. Jack and I were quiet and ate with our eyes down, overawed by the dark room and the table in a pool of light. At the end of the meal the adults pushed back their chairs.

The two men in their shirt sleeves, the two women in their flowered dresses, clustered at the front door... 'Come out to see us, won't you, " Arthur said, ' New Jersey isn't the end of the world you know. He put out his hand and my father shook it.

My father said heartily, 'Of course we will!' You can count on it.

trauma

in my parents'
lives

was what
they called
hard luck

to my mother

from my father
'wedding day, 1925'

'I know you will be
a good and obedient wife'
Found in her prayer book

Then May told my mother she'd miss her and they hugged, awkwardly, just their cheeks touching.   While all the hugging and handshaking and promises were going on Jack started upstairs. I saw him slide out our hall door and into the shadowy hallway.and vanish up the dark stairwell. He hadn't waved and he hadn't said goodbye but he was going. In fact, he was gone.

Something Falling

I saw the shadow of something falling
As if from the tree to the grass

And I wondered if it were a bird
Or maybe a shadow

That looked like a bird
That had the shape a bird needs

To surf the skies-
But no hardiness yet in the wings

Now I think it was
a fledgling love

That tried the air
And fell to earth

Before it knew
the strength it takes to fly

Easter

little girl
in her smart new coat

shivers
a flower
blooming early

Eventually, it seemed like a very long time later, the promise made to Jack's parents was kept; we were going to visit them in their new house, their house with a lawn, somewhere in the next State. My father borrowed an automobile from a friend. The car had a rumble seat, an uncovered passenger seat that folded out from the rear of the car. That's where my little sister and I would travel. We left so early in the morning you could still see the ghost of stars in the pearl-coloured sky. Pat and I settled into the rumble seat, with an old grey lap robe over our knees and a packet of sandwiches at our feet. We clung to each other, rising with the bumps, swaying around the corners, our lives going off track in the most exciting way.

filling the dog's bowl

water spills over
the vessel too small

to hold
so much
love

Jack had a dog, a longhaired black dog that sometimes showed some of its teeth as if it were smiling. It ran along behind him. He took his dog for a walk that afternoon and I was allowed to go with him. We went into a woods, dappled light coming through green overarching trees. There was a stream, clear water rippling over stones. There were bushes with blackberries on them. Jack gathered some and gave them to me, from his warm cupped hand to mine.

We were walking along the pathway next to the stream, the dog splashing in the water, when Jack suddenly sprinted ahead. He'd spotted a tiny bird lying under a tree. It had almost no feathers and looked like a fallen leaf among other fallen leaves to me, but he had seen it. It was a fledgling with a broken wing.

on a wall

near the prattling stream
a wild rose

silently
listens
and learns

Gently, he carried the fledgling home. Up in his room he made a nest for it, tearing up newspaper to line a cardboard shoebox he took out of his closet.

He put the bird in the box and the box on the chest of drawers-. His bedroom furniture had a Mexican design on it: a peon asleep by a cactus with his sombrero over his eyes. Jack said he would feed the bird grubs. Later I heard the wing had mended and he had set the bird free.

Years would pass and a war would be fought and won before I saw Jack again. Maybe by then I had made up the ending myself.

telling him

I loved him
when I was young

the truth
but not
the whole truth

Reaching New Jersey

Towards the end of a 1930's summer
my father, a land-locked sailor,
borrowed a Model A Ford to drive us to a friend's house.
He would navigate by the sun, he said,
New Jersey's North by West from Brooklyn.
A passenger seat folded out from the trunk of the car,
its lid the back we leaned against, my sister and I,
 a roofless rumble seat... like an open boat.
Her warm arm linked with mine
our bare knees cold under a thin blanket
we were weightless with joy heading for New Jersey.
We sailed past a highway's billboards
tacked to a dust-choked road
before, at some sudden crossroads,
launching again on the startled highway.
That night a padlocked chain fence barred the way
behind it, black water heaved like a slumbering animal.
We parked on the lap of a fruitless fruit stand
and chastened, slept under silent staring stars.
Morning lit our friend's house and the road across the reservoir.
Later I'd forget if I had doubted in the dark
Recalling only faith, when I was young,
that with the sun to lead we'd reach New Jersey.
It was the only mapless journey I would know
Except, of course, for love.

A Casualty

The day after Pearl Harbor
his whole basketball team signed up

so he did too
because that was one sure way

to get out of going to school
And the Marines

taught him
everything he needed to know

to become a sniper
and a scout

before sending him
to Iwo Jima

where he was taught
to spray the caves with fire

to force the enemy to come out
which they did

including one very young soldier,
 just a boy,

in flames.
And the only thing

he could't learn
was how to live with that.

for a glimpse

of him returning
I wait

a shadow
in
an open door

In April,1945, Hitler committed suicide and in May the Germans surrendered. Huge crowds celebrated in London but America was still in mourning for Franklin Delano Roosevelt who'd led us through the war and died before he could see this happen. Flags were sat half-mast for FDR, but huge crowds packed in to Times Square to cheer and sing anyway.

The war that was ended in Europe wasn't my war. My war was where Jack was, in the Pacific with the Third Marine Corps. The Third Marines served in the battles of Bougainville, Guam and finally Iwo Jima . Those were the battles I read about in the newspapers. Those were the newsreels I scanned hoping to see his face among the boatloads of young Marines heading for the landing beaches.. I made cookies and sent them to him packed in my old school lunchbox. I bought a miraculous medal for him and had our initials engraved on it.

I posted it to him and no one could stop me -because there was a war on.

Later, on Iwo Jima, there would be no 'battle lines'. There, the Marines were in the open and the Japanese were entrenched below ground, firing at them, hidden in a web of tunnels- that stretched underground for 18 km. Riflemen like Jack were issued with portable flame throwers - a tank holding 18 litres of gasoline, worn on the back, a pressure tank and a flame gun. Their orders were to flush the Japanese from their caves and pillboxes. For the rest of his life, Jack had one recurring nightmare. He wouldn't talk about it. He grew very angry if you mentioned it. He was still seeing a young Japanese soldier engulfed in flames.

The battle went on from February 19 to March 26ᵗʰ 1945. When the island was secured, Jack was sent home for his first period of 'rest and recuperation' in four years. Nobody knew when he would arrive. As it happened, he reached the west coast of the USA four months later, on the day the war ended. News of victory in Japan on 14 August 1945 really did spark an explosion of joy in the USA. The war was really, finally over.

Jack called in to visit us one evening. We didn't know he had returned; we hadn't known he was coming. My sister happened to look out the window as a black convertible pulled up to the curb; she saw Jack get out in his Marine uniform and she shouted the news to the household. Jack was there. He was thin but his uniform stretched over his shoulders tightly. His cap was tucked into his belt. His red hair was darker now more like mahogany, and still curly despite the military haircut. He greeted all of us as we clustered excitedly at the door. His brown eyes were more wary than when he'd been a kid, but his smile was as warm as ever.

It was a smile that lit up his face and invited you to be happy too. But Jack had only called in to say hello. Once again he was gone.

time passes
leaving questions
unanswered

looking for a pattern
in a shuffled
pack of cards

Would he ever get in touch with me again?   It became less likely every day. The boys were returning and there was a panic like a rumble of thunder. Hurry , time to get married , time to start a family. His mother told mine that Jack was living with his father on a farm in Virginia. Eventually, I stopped even dreaming that Jack would come back for me.

In 1947, I was 21 and most girls of 21 were married. The boys being sent back to civilian life were 24 or 25. We had never been 'teenagers'. We had lived through a war, and we were adults.

I met Robert at his coming-home party when he was demobbed from the army. He too was ready to start a life with a home of his own. It was flattering to be chosen and romantic to be courted with daily notes and phone calls snatched on office time.

Sometimes, last thing at night, Jack's face, his smile, would come into my mind for a moment, but what good was that to me now? I hadn't seen him for two years.The choice was between a dream and reality. The adult choice was surely 'reality'. I might never see Jack again while Robert was someone who looked forward to sharing his life with me, who was available, persistent and very sure I was the one he wanted.

We married and our child was born that year. A difficult birth, it would be our only child. A girl. I was happy to have a daughter but Robert was deeply disappointed . We named the baby Roberta . She was 14 years old when Robert and I divorced .

flying down

through storm-tumbled
clouds

landing safely
sweet sound
of rain

just as I accept

tomorrow
is another day

I see
the problem
with that

Fifteen years after I'd last seen Jack, I phoned him. I was on a business trip to Washington to attend.a meeting . I knew he lived in Virginia. and he was listed in the phone book.. I dialled and he answered...I recognised his voice after all that time. Bright, friendly. 'This is Jack,' he said.. I'll be right there!' It was so unexpected. it made me laugh. 'But you don't even know who this is!' I said.

-      'Doesn't matter who it is,' he answered. 'I'll be right there!'.. And as if an after thought- 'Who is it?'

-      Maryalicia –

-      'Where are you?

I gave him the name and the address of the hotel and , again, no question.. no 'what are you doing there'. He just said - I'll be there in an hour', and hung up , as if in a hurry to be on his way, not to keep me wait today.

today

to prove I'm alive
I'll throw a pebble

in the ocean
and start
a ripple

ambushed by spring

cherry blossoms
telling me

winter is over
when it yet
may snow

I sat in the lobby and watched the clock. I knew I was smiling. Forty-five minutes later, Jack walked into the lobby. He was wearing blue jeans and a denim work shirt, a lit cigarette was cupped in his hand.. He wasn't the red headed boy of 30 years ago, or the young Marine either. He was broader, filled out, but still slim. His hair had darkened and was receding at the temples. . His face was brown so his freckles didn't stand out the way they used to. His sleeves, turned back, showed wrists as strong as I remembered them and the familiar square workman-like hands. I crossed to the reception desk and reached it just as he did and standing next to him, I said hello. He turned his face towards my voice and smiled. His eyes were the same warm brown, his smile as bright..

'Great you showed up out here, ' he said. He meant at the desk. "I didn't know who to ask the desk clerk for.. I couldn't remember your last name."

What would you have done"?

'I'd have phoned my mother and asked her.' He was laughing. "She's in Paris…"

After that I could think of nothing to say. We were standing face to face in the hotel lobby now. I was aware of the scene, the swirls of green on the carpet, the rust coloured upholstered couch, us in the centre of the abandoned the meeting without a qualm.

"Would you like to see the farm?" he asked. Without a second thought for the meeting which was assembling behind me, I said yes. We walked out, side by side in the spring sunshine, to his car.

If I could have you back ..

If I could have you back my friend
I'd waste no time in sorrow
Accept that even good things end.

If I could have you back my friend
I'd use each day that fate might send
Storing joy to light tomorrow,

If I could have you back my friend
I'd waste no time in sorrow

each day

birds circle the sky
restless-

restless til twilight
when they fly home

Jack's house was three stories high, built of cream coloured stone; the windows, geometrically positioned, were flanked with white wooden shutters. It was a facade like a child's geometric drawing of a house. Old magnolia trees with large pink blossoms stood on either side of the house,   black-green boxwood hedges bordered the formal gravel path that led to the steps to the front door. The date 1832 was carved over the side door that led into the gunroom. This was more like a living room, though in this house the formal living room was upstairs . There were guns on racks against the wall and a glass-fronted cabinet held more. The floors were of narrow red bricks covered partially by a silky red Chinese carpet. There was an oil painting of an18th century farmyard on one wall and opposite it a stone fireplace so enormous I could have stood up straight inside of it. A Japanese battle flag hung, framed, near the door.

What now, on this unlooked for day, a day with an empty seat in a conference room where I should have been, a day in the company of a man I had loved for so long but who wouldn't love me?-

'We could go for a walk in the Blue Ridge Mountains if you'd like,' Jack offered. - "Okay,' I said .' But would you think there's anything else around here I could wear?' I was in a tailored dress in black and white checks and high heeled shoes.

Jack went off immediately to find something, just as if he were helping me out in a dressing-up child's game.. He came back with a pair of his jeans. a checkered shirt and a pair of flip-flops. I put them on in the bathroom next to the gunroom, leaving my stockings and high heels behind with my dress. I came out with one hand holding up the trousers. Jack had a necktie ready to cinch up the trousers around my waist.

He said I looked 'perfect'.. .

We drove to the mountains. "There's a great view from a place at the top," Jack said. "We could watch the sunset."   It was   steep, circuitous route and I climbed it almost bent in two, flip-flops beating against the soles of my feet.. We reached a large flat rock set in a clearing. It was like a theatre seat. Below us were the darkly wooded slopes of the mountain, and beside us the scrubby bushes that grew at this elevation, stunted in the wind. In front of us, the view stretched out like a map of the world.. The sun was a big bronze disk low in the sky. We watched it silently, waiting for it to fall behind the horizon. But instead it dropped into a cloud like a penny in a slot and at once the day grew dark.

It was suddenly cold. We stayed where we were.

"Is there a husband waiting to spring out from behind a bush?" Jack asked me then. I said no. I told him my marriage was over and I was working as a journalist, making a life for my daughter and myself.

It was getting darker and we started down the mountain .The last few yards he went ahead to find the way, and I ran the last few steps. He had turned to wait for me and it was tempting to run into his arms but I didn't. I stopped so close I could see the stitches in his sweater and feel the warmth from his body.

"They have a restaurant down here, " he said. And so they did, but through the glass door I could see nicely dressed couples dining by candlelight. I couldn't brave it in my tramp costume.

"Okay," he said,"we'll go the Dairy Queen". We drove into town to a stand run by an elderly lady Jack had known for years. She was delighted to see him and tried not to stare at me. He told her he'd found me by the side of the road and I was hungry. Instantly sympathetic, she poured out a glass of milk for me and another for Jack and prepared a plate of 'ham biscuits' for us both., salty baked Virginia ham between slices of buttered baking powder biscuits.

It was late when we got back to the farm and we went straight through to the kitchen. Jack flicked on one overhead light, crossed over to the green tile counter top and began to make two mugs of instant coffee. I waited leaning against the wall just inside the door. We were at the far sides of a big room and I couldn't bring myself to bridge the physical gap.

I listen

the wind
is sharing a secret

too late
it's something
I already know

After coffee, Jack had seen me to a guest room, kissed me quickly on the cheek and left. This morning, following the scent of coffee, I found him in the gunroom having his breakfast from the coffee table. I sat on the couch next to him and he asked how I'd slept.

'Never better," I told him honestly. A maid came in to the room. He introduced her to me. ''Mary Frances' wore a pale green uniform with a white collar and a white apron. Like Miss Jenny in the Dairy Queen, Mary Frances tried hard not to stare but her alert eyes kept sliding back to me.

Over breakfast, Jack and I talked about what we'd do with the day.My going to the meeting wasn't mentioned. We went for a walk around the farm. A river formed one boundary. A Civil War battle had been fought here and the ruins of an old mill crumbled into the mud at the water's edge. The shore was rocky and slippery and Jack took my hand. Our walk took us along the edge of a small woods where violets grew under the slender trees and though the going was good again, he still kept my hand in his.   We passed a pond with a rowboat in it, and a cluster of farm worker's buildings. The day slid by.

That evening, we drove to a roadside restaurant . It was dark when we got back and the farm manager had lit the fire in the big gunroom fireplace. The logs were still blazing. We sat on the carpet in front of it and watched the flames dance. Our shoulders touched and we turned towards each other. It was like being nineteen again except I was older and wiser and knew enough to live for the moment.

snow fall

on red
holly berries

his cheek
on mine
the first time

Six weeks later we were married by Rob Roy, Justice of the Peace. Mrs. Roy played 'Oh promise me' on the organ in their tidy sitting room – with its lace curtains and potted ferns – and then Mr. Roy read out the marriage ceremony. Jack read it over his shoulder to be sure of coming in on time with his 'I do'. He said the words in such a heartfelt way the hackneyed phrase sounded new-minted.

When Roberta's school term was over I handed in the keys to my apartment and we three drove down to Virginia from New York. It was warm and sunny, the middle of June. We turned into the long driveway and crested the first hill. Before us, we could see the farmhouse, our new home. We were like survivors of a ship wreck with the shore in sight: a 39 year old ex- bachelor, his new wife and her 14 year old daughter, whom he'd met only six weeks ago.

blue green

like water
like the mediterranean

the stone
in the ring
he gave me

Jack played golf with the local trades people he had come to call his friends, the electricians, insurance salesmen, lawyers and bakers he knew from his rounds in town. He had invited them to the farm for their holidays and they didn't change their plans just because Jack was married now. Jack and I found some time for ourselves in the eye of the storm...driving together to the market for food or the hardware shop for pool supplies.

It was horse country and Jack bought me a hunter. In the autumn I'd join a decorous Virginia hunt. Preparing for my debut I rode every corner of our 600 acres, practicing jumps over our rail walls.

We slept out on a screened in porch on the second floor; sometimes, in his sleep, Jack shouted out 'get down, get down,' and pressed me down with his arm across my chest. The memory of Iwo Jima was still not erased and maybe never would be.

Twice he'd been buried alive there- once in an explosion -another by a collapsing cave. And twice he'd been dug out by fellow Marines. Both time he'd seen a light filled tunnel and longed to follow it. Each time a voice had turned him back.

even now

when the wind
rises

I reach
for his hand
forgetting

Cross Country

We don't meet as equals this horse and I
Our relationship already framed by his training
Was it harsh?
He accepts -
accepts my encumbering saddle upon his back
and the bit in his mouth
not kicking, not bucking, not taking flight
but enduring.
Holding his instincts in check
against myriad irritations
as only the most noble can do
until my legs and hands
and the balance of my body
signal I mean no harm
Then, in exchange for that small civility,
he lends me his strength
his heart and his courage
sharing the best that he is
so I can be more than I am
for a little while
cross country.

We knew the farm would have to be sold sooner or later. Arthur had bought it and willed it to Jack, a millionaire's house that needed a millionaire 's purse to run. Five years later, the time had come and the estate was sold to a conglomerate of New York business men.

One day, looking about for the last time, I opened a cupboard in a seldom used room. On the top shelf , there was a familiar green box . It was like glimpsing the face of a friend in a crowd on a foreign street. My school lunch box, the one I'd filled with cookies and shipped off to Jack in the South Pacific seventeen years ago.

Lifting the battered lid I found inside, wedged in the corner, the miraculous medal with our initials engraved on it.

I asked him about them that evening.. I said I was surprised he still had them.

'Do you think you were the only one who could love so much?' he asked me.

And I said 'yes'.

some nights

my soul
goes searching

for memories
I've left
in old rooms

My sister and her husband had rented an old manor house in Sligo
on the west shore of Ireland and we had agreed to visit. We sailed to
Ireland on a ship of the Holland America Line .

Jack packed a new tuxedo and I had three new evening gowns.

We danced on the deck in the moonlight .

slanting sun

late afternoon
I remember

living in your light
and how slowly
evening fell

Souvenir

A box stencilled with flowers
and the name of a town in white –
Santa Margherita de Ligure-
failed souvenir of a village
sun-pinned to a hill
I have forgotten it all
Not a single shop, cafe, street
do I remember.
I close my eyes
and see only the shape
of your body bending
to the boy selling mementos
the light behind you
as you turn back to me
putting this box in my hands
gently as if it were fragile or I was
and the challenge in your eyes
that I would meet each night
until our nights ran out.

Self-portrait with rainbow

Was it a coincidence
That caught the artist
In a rainbow
With her eyes wide
To all the colours
In her hair

Or did a fixed appointment
Lead her step by step
With her canvas
To the old place
Where the rainbow
Waited for her

We arrived in Ireland, offloaded from the liner at Cobh. Once through the customs shed we huddled in the doorway of a shuttered shop waiting for the car we'd hired to to meet us. We had very little luggage. In addition to some clothes, I brought for safe keeping the tin lunch box with the medal still inside and my saddle. I'd learned to ride on the farm and was looking forward to some outings in Ireland,. The breeze was blowing stiffly. We watched the wind-blown litter drift down the grey street to lodge in sheltered corners.

We had no timetable to follow, no return ticket. For guidance we had Ireland on Five Dollars a Day and Muirheads' Blue Book of Ireland.. When we finally set off from Cobh we had an outline plan, of visiting Cork, Limerick and Sligo then flying back to the States.

On the map the distances looked short but the roads were narrow and twisting . It could take us most of the day to find a destination only 30 miles distant, rolling along like a bowling ball between curved alleys of high walls and blind hedges . The sun appeared from time to time like a rationed commodity. The cities when we reached them seemed oddly similar, low buildings darkened with soot.

Soon we learned the better way was to fold the map and head nowhere in particular. These were the days that held us. End of season Americans, we were like off-course migratory birds and the old man we'd stop on the road for directions or the woman who'd sell us an airmail stamp from her shop-post office-pub would stretch out a conversation like a staying hand to keep us in view. Would we know Jimmy McNamara in New Jersey? No? We'd be told his story anyway.

Often we'd drive on with the light hearted feeling of having been offered much more than we'd asked for, certainly given much more than we'd bought. And we'd be carried along through the fading afternoon by our own rare sightings – a watercolour vista of green fields gilded by the slanting sun, revised by rain, or a purple shop front framed in a fuchsia hedge. Not too many days later we looked out on the foaming Atlantic from Sligo's cliffs and could hardly remember crossing it.

we stood

on Sligo's boney shoulders
looking down on the frothy sea

the sea
we crossed
to find home

After Sligo, we set off for the east coast of Ireland . Roberta and Miss Jenny's daughter Judy (who'd become her best friend)were cycling through Europe. We rented a cottage in a Wicklow town called Ashford. The town had a bridge and a stream and looked like a Hollywood stage set. The cottage itself was on a hilly unpaved road and across from it an estate was hidden behind trees and encircled with an iron fence. It was a hotel . The owner's daughter kept a stable of horses for hire. I began to ride 'greener' horses than I'd ever known over greener fields than I'd ever imagined

New friends, fellow riders, asked us to dinners where the ladies wore long skirts and there was an astonishing amount of cutlery on the table. We found out what' party pieces' were, and that we didn't have any and that it didn't matter. The others had enough songs and stories to make any evening last until morning.

Meanwhile, our temporary entry permits were expiring. We presented ourselves at the Garda Station and became registered aliens. We were given little green cards that said we could stay 'without condition as to time', an apt description of our visit so far.

balancing on her shadow

a woman walks
into her future

the sun on her back
if it rains
she will see a rainbow

We acquired a cat. .. a thick-coated grey female that showed up one morning and never left, more or less the way we had arrived in Dublin ourselves. We called her Kitty. A neighbour's aloof, tough male cat was named Parnell, so our Kitty became Kitty O'Shea. They sat side by side on the wall in the sun in the morning, the tips of their tails interlocked.

One Monday morning, I saw an advertisement in the Irish Times for a 2CV. I'd heard Jack admiring these eccentric-looking little cars, the Citroen 2CV.. He never asked for anything, never seemed to want anything. This was my chance to do something special for him. The advertisement listed a work number for a contact so well before office hours -at eight in the morning-, in fact, I rang the number and let it ring. I tied the line up until the phone was answered at 9:30 .

'I could hear the phone ringing from the car park," the man who answered said. He was out of breath.

'I was just ringing to tell you your car is sold " I told him. 'Name your price.'

The seller was astonished - and though he could have asked almost anything he wanted, so determined was I to surprise Jack with this car —he quoted a very reasonable figure. The job was done. Jack was as delighted as I'd hoped he'd be. On the day he collected it he drove it around for hours. Very soon, the car became almost a family pet, like a pony or a dog. The neighbourhood children learned to drive in it, cruising up and down the lane sitting on Jack's knee, steering while he worked the pedals. When they grew older, they pushed the pedals for themselves.

each autumn

my old cat
learns anew

blowing leaves
are only
leaves blowing

In our 2 cv we travelled Europe, too.Before Irish ferries became more sophisticated, the 2cv would be driven on to a net dockside and lifted on to the ship in its cradle. From France we'd journey on to Italy, to Germany, then home again- always happy to be back.

Jack acquired a Dragon, a wooden-hulled boat made in Norway and sailed competitively . Winters, he followed the hunt, watching out for sightings of me. Only three times did I fail to appear; once I'd broken a leg a few fields back ,another time my horse had broken a leg and I'd waited sobbing until a vet could come and put her down. The third time I had had a fall and was concussed. As Irish hunting went, this wasn't a bad record.

I was happy

sleeping in his arms
waking to his voice

never noticing the clock
and how quickly
the hands move

Just before Christmas we moved up from the country to a house in Dublin. It was a mews, once a stable and carriage house belonging to the Georgian house whose rear facade rose four stories high at the end of the garden. The stable had been awkwardly refitted into a small dwelling with a neglected patch of ground behind it where roses clung to leggy bushes even in winter.   It was still more closely related to a stable than a house, with wrought iron rings embedded in the stone walls in what was now our sitting room. Once the rings had been where four carriage horses were tethered. High gates hid the dwelling from the back lane that serviced it.

We tied a holly wreath on our gate but took it down when a neighbour called to say people would think 'those nice Americans' had a death in the family. We ordered a turkey and its inseparable companion, the ham, forfeited sweet potatoes and came to terms with sprouts. There were no cranberries.We squinted in the smoke of a tiny turf fire and reminded ourselves that in Virginia at Christmas it would be snowing. In fact, when people asked us what had brought us to Ireland, Jack always said it was the climate and they laughed.

Jack, who always had a project going in the house, had to learn a new vocabulary now.. Not Irish -which most of our new friends had used at school but none used in daily life - but new words in English for ordinary things.. our 'hardware store' was now the ironmongers, faucets were 'taps' ' 'baseboards' had become 'skirting boards', even the first floor in a house became the hall floor while the first floor was now the second floor. Jack was good at pantomime and his shopping trips made him even better.

Imperceptibly,   new friends became old friends. Their recommendations guided us from doctor, to dentist to solicitor to bank- it was like belonging to a big family. We never thought any more of going 'home', except if we were referring to Dublin. Jack carved our initials- JP MH and a heart on our garden wall.

    sunlight

    turning green leaves
    gold

    then red
    soon they will drift down
    briefly glorious

Ordinary Days

I give thanks for ordinary days..
not birthdays, holidays, red letter days

but days when I'm not waiting
for anything

and nothing
is waiting for me

ordinary days
that start with coffee

from a big cup
at my kitchen table

days I watch birds come and go
on the tree outside the window

and listen to the
old dog's muffled snores

as she sleeps on her cushion
near the fire

and I know all I need
to make me happy

I have right now-
this ordinary day

One night Jack woke with a pain in his back. He stood by the bed and twisted his arm behind him to put a thumb on the spot.. just above his waist.'What do you think that is?" he asked. I didn't know.

He couldn't sleep any more that night and neither could I. I lay waiting for the sun to rise so I could ring the doctor. When the doctor came he gave him something for pain but over the day the pain grew worse . That night the doctor sent him to hospital 'for tests'.

The next morning he gave us the news.

'This was truly serendipitous! " he said. "' The pain will go.. .. it was probably a touch of food poisoning. But the ex-ray showed up a tumour in the lung. We'd never have known it was there if he hadn't had that pain.

'And it's in a good place, "he added enthusiastically. " Just where we like to see them. Easy to reach. We'll operate after Christmas.. go home and have a good holiday."

hello love

the postman said
as people here

still sometimes do
how could he know
I needed that today

In this old country
leaves die quietly
come autumn
not screaming red
the way they do
where I was born

We did have a good holiday and joked about the surgeon's mournful sounding 'good wishes'.   Now, the holidays were over and Jack was back in hospital. Surgery had been ruled out, the cancer having 'galloped away from them.'   Chemotherapy was making him ill, doing more harm than good they said, so it was ruled out too.

Jack had relays of visitors – friends, neighbours, the children of friends and neighbours. Jack made an effort to respond to them but it was exhausting for him. The hospital moved him to a private room but in fact, hospital itself was tiring with its rota of room cleaners and newspaper sellers and the occasional nun stopping by to say a prayer.

It would be better for Jack if I took him home .

visitors

surge
around hospital beds

tide ebbs
silence
like empty sea shells

The hospice would help me. There would be someone show me what I had to do. The move felt urgent. I asked the nurse in the station at the end of the hall for the hospice phone number. I would see how quickly we could move Jack. I reached for the phone and the nurse put her hand on mine .

"Aren't we taking good care of him here ? ' she asked very gently. And then she said it:

'He only has two days left in him."

listen

a child
 is crying

maybe
it's
me

comforter

the quilt
that warms me

now that he
is never
coming back

I hadn't wanted to know .. I had asked the doctor not to tell me and the nurses knew that too. But now that death was so near, knowing was alright. It gave me only a few hours to live through, vividly aware that the hours were trickling away like a sand in an hour glass turned for the last time. The nurse patted my shoulder and I went back to Jack's room.

That night he fell into a deep sleep after the morphine injection that dulled his pain without ever erasing it entirely,. His face was gaunt, his cheekbones stuck out. He hadn't eaten since the chemo had made him sick.

Dear God, I wondered, how dead do you have to be before you die? I moistened his lips with the water the nurse brought me.

not wanting to leave
I left
 this morning
milk in the tea
clouded
the tea leaves

In the dim cold light thrown into the room by a nearby streetlight, I packed his bag. It was the bag in which he used to carry his change of clothes when he went out sailing. Dry clothes for the drive home.

Now I was using it to pack the pyjamas I'd bought him for this hospital stay, the fresh tee shirts, the shaving kit, its leather worn from the touch of his hand. It felt like giving up, and it was. Death had already claimed him, it was just waiting to take him away. Tomorrow he would be gone and the bed would be needed for someone else.

Through that night, each time the bells tolled the hours from the church around the corner, I stroked Jack's arm. I reasoned that what worked for Pavlov's dogs would work for me. So I memorised the feeling of his skin, of the hair on his skin, the warmth of his arm. The tolling of bells brings the warmth of him back to me even now.

It was the last night I would watch him sleep.

if I stopped coping

let the tears
slide down

who would
sing me to sleep?

In the morning, Jack opened his eyes and looked at me for the last time. He tried to cup my face in his hands but he was too weak and his hands slipped back. I held them against my cheeks for him, my hands over his. .

"I'm dying, ' he said. He sounded not sad, but surprised. "Yes my love," I said. "Yes you are."

We'd had our miracles, there were to be no more.. Against the odds we'd had thirty years together .

I didn't beg him to stay, to fight, to hold on. He had no choice. It was time for him to journey on. A tear slid down his cheek and I kissed it away. I knew that he'd soon see that tunnel , the one he'd seen on Iwo Jima. Then he'd longed to see where it led .This time he wouldn't be turned back.

'Go to the light,' I whispered, " You can go the end of the tunnel now'.

His eyes were closed, his lips barely moving...'My loyal friend' he said . His soul left him softly. .

***

sleepless night

shadow
of a silent tree

waiting
for the sound of birds
morning

    I hear you

    say my name
    in dreams

    each night
    a moment's hope
    before truth dawns

And One Day

And one day
Will it just stop
A final gurgle and all over
All my lessons
All my love
Lost?
Better still
I will believe
They'll bounce
Up to the sky
Where, kept intact,
They'll wait
Until a celestial download
Automatically
Fills my heart
With them again
For the next life .